A Note to Parents and Teachers

DK READERS is a compelling program for beginning readers, designed in conjunction with leading literacy experts, including Dr. Linda Gambrell, director of the Eugene T. Moore School of Education, Clemson University, and past president of the National Reading Conference.

Beautiful illustrations and superb full-color photographs combine with engaging, easy-to-read stories to offer a fresh approach to each subject in the series. Each DK READER is guaranteed to capture a child's interest while developing his or her reading skills, general knowledge, and love of reading.

The four levels of DK READERS are aimed at different reading abilities, enabling you to choose the books that are exactly right for your child:

Level 1 — Beginning to read
Level 2 — Beginning to read alone
Level 3 — Reading alone
Level 4 — Proficient reader

The "normal" age at which a child begins to read can be anywhere from three to eight years old, so these levels are only a general guideline.

No matter which level you select, you can be sure that you are helping your child learn to read, then read to learn!

LONDON, NEW YORK, MELBOURNE,
MUNICH, AND DELHI

Senior Editor Beth Sutinis
Senior Art Editor Michelle Baxter
Publisher Chuck Lang
Creative Director Tina Vaughan
Production Chris Avgherinos

Reading Consultant
Linda Gambrell, Ph.D.

Produced by NFL Creative
Editorial Director John Wiebusch
Managing Editor John Fawaz
Art Director Evelyn Javier

First American Edition, 2003

03 04 05 10 9 8 7 6 5 4 3 2 1
Published in the United States by DK Publishing, Inc.
375 Hudson Street, New York, New York 10014

ISBN: 0-7894-9865-0 (PB)
ISBN: 0-7894-9864-2 (HC)

A Catalog Record is available from the Library of Congress.

Color reproduction by Asia Pacific
Printed and bound in China
by L. Rex Printing Co., Ltd.

Photography credits:
t=top, b=below, l=left, r=right, c=center,
Vernon Biever 13, 36br, 41bc; David Boss 5bl; Rob Brown 35tr;
Jimmy Cribb 9c; Malcolm Emmons 19tr, 24br, 42bc;
James Flores 4tl, 6tl; Rod Hanna 15tr; Fred Kaplan 38br;
Allen Kee 40, 42tl, 43; Richard Mackson 26, 30bc;
Al Messerschmidt 21, 23br, 24tl, 32bc, 34bl, 45;
NFL Photos 6bc, 15bc, 16, 17tr; Darryl Norenberg 10, 14;
Al Pereira 38tl; Robert Riger 7tl; Bob Rosato 30tl, 36tl;
George Rose 28tl, 34tl; Manny Rubio 19c, 25, 27bc;
Bill Smith 22, 28bc; James D. Smith 37; Paul Spinelli/NFLP front
cover left, 2, 3, 23bl, 33br, 33tl, 39, 44, 46bc, 47;
David Stluka 35tl; Tony Tomsic front cover right, 11br, 12br, 18;
Michael Zagaris 20, 27tr, 41tr; John Zimmerman 17lc;

Discover more at
www.dk.com

Contents

NFL

SUPER BOWL!

Written by Tim Polzer

DK Publishing, Inc.

Max McGee

SUPER BOWL I
January 15, 1967
Memorial Coliseum
Los Angeles,
California
Green Bay Packers 35
Kansas City Chiefs 10

Green Bay
quarterback Bart
Starr completed 16
of 23 passes for 250
yards and 2 scores to
lead the Packers to
a 35–10 victory over
Kansas City in
Super Bowl I.
Little-used Green
Bay receiver Max
McGee, who
replaced injured
starter Boyd Dowler,
caught 7 passes for
138 yards and 2
touchdown passes.
Starr was named the
game's most
valuable player.

Birth of the Super Bowl

During the National Football League's first 13 seasons (1920–1932), the team with the best record was named champion. There were no playoff games after the season ended.

Beginning in 1933, the 10 NFL teams split into Eastern and Western Divisions, and the two division winners played each other in the NFL Championship Game.

That's the way things stayed until the 1960s, when the American

AFL Logo

NFL Logo (1960)

Football League came along. The AFL, which started in 1960, competed with the NFL for players, fans, and money from television networks that paid to broadcast games. After six years of costly battles, the NFL and AFL

4

decided to merge into one league.

On June 8, 1966, NFL Commissioner Pete Rozelle announced that the two leagues would merge in 1970. But fans wouldn't have to wait that long to find out which league was better.

That's because the AFL and NFL agreed to a game matching the champions of each league. The first one was scheduled for January 1967, after the conclusion of the 1966 season. That contest, then called the AFL-NFL World Championship Game, soon came to be known as the Super Bowl.

With only seven months to prepare, the first AFL-NFL Championship Game had to be planned in a

Pete Rozelle

Empty Seats
While 61,946 people attended Super Bowl I, there were more than 30,000 empty seats in the huge Los Angeles Memorial Coliseum. It was the only Super Bowl that did not sell out.

Lombardi Trophy
The prize awarded to Super Bowl champions is called the Lombardi Trophy. It is named in honor of Green Bay coach Vince Lombardi, whose Packers won Super Bowls I and II. Under Lombardi, the Packers won five NFL championships in seven seasons (1961–67).

Bart Starr

SUPER BOWL II
January 14, 1968
Orange Bowl
Miami, Florida
Green Bay Packers 33
Oakland Raiders 14

After defeating Dallas in the legendary Ice Bowl to claim the NFL championship, the Packers met the Oakland Raiders in Super Bowl II.

Green Bay jumped to a 13–0 lead that was reduced to 16–7 at halftime. The Packers put away the game in the second half, capped by Herb Adderley's 60-yard interception return for a touchdown.

Bart Starr completed 13 of 24 passes for 202 yards and a touchdown to win his second Super Bowl MVP award.

hurry. When those plans were complete, the Kansas City Chiefs of the AFL and the Green Bay Packers of the NFL met at a neutral site, the Los Angeles Memorial Coliseum, on January 15, 1967, in the first Super Bowl.

That game confirmed what many fans believed: That the older, established NFL, stocked with veteran

Vince Lombardi

Kansas City Chiefs

players, was better than the AFL.

Under the direction of legendary coach Vince Lombardi, the Packers scored the game's first touchdown and never trailed. They led only 14–10 at halftime, but exploded in the second half and scored 3 touchdowns.

Green Bay's 35–10 victory gave the NFL bragging rights over the AFL. When asked about the Chiefs, Lombardi said, "They don't even rate with the top teams in our division."

Winners' Ring
Each player on the winning Super Bowl team receives a Super Bowl ring. Green Bay's rings for Super Bowl I were made of sterling silver and featured a diamond in the crown.

Game Program
The *Official Super Bowl Game Program* offers team rosters, feature stories, and scouting reports to help fans enjoy the game. The cover price of the Super Bowl I game program was $1. The Super Bowl XXXVII program cost $18.

How the Game Has Grown

The first Super Bowl was not as popular as the game is today. The differences between Super Bowl I in 1967 and Super Bowl XXXVII in 2003 are stunning.

For instance, the most expensive tickets for Super Bowl I cost $12. Many fans thought the price was too high, and more than 30,000 tickets went unsold (it was the only Super Bowl that did not sell out). Tickets for Super Bowl XXXVII cost as much as $500, and some fans were willing to pay many times that.

Green Bay players earned $15,000 each for winning Super Bowl I. Kansas City players each received a losing share of $7,500. Thirty-six years later, Tampa Bay players each earned $63,000 for winning Super Bowl XXXVII, and Oakland players received $35,000.

Thousands of members of the media report on each Super Bowl.

Ticket Prices

The cost of a Super Bowl ticket has risen since Super Bowl I. Here are ticket price ranges for the first 37 games:

I: $12, $10, $6
II–III: $12
IV–VIII: $15
IX–XI: $20
XII–XIV: $30
XV–XVII: $40
XVIII–XIX: $60
XX–XXI: $75
XXII–XXIII: $100
XXIV: $125
XXV–XXVI: $150
XXVII–XXVIII: $175
XXIX: $200
XXX: $350, $250, $200
XXXI–XXXII: $275
XXXIII–XXXV: $325
XXXVI: $400
XXXVII: $500, $400

Just 338 media passes were issued to the first Super Bowl. More than 3,000 media passes were issued for Super Bowl XXXVII.

Approximately 85 million people in two countries watched the television broadcast of Super Bowl I. More than 800 million people in 165 countries watched Super Bowl XXXVII on television.

The cost of a 30-second television commercial during Super Bowl I was $42,000. The cost to air a 30-second commercial during Super Bowl XXXVII was more than $2 million.

Because Super Bowl television audiences have become so large, advertisers try to create especially memorable commercials for the

Receiver Otis Taylor (89) caught a 46-yard touchdown pass from Len Dawson, and running back Mike Garrett (21) scored on a 5-yard run in Super Bowl IV.

Even the President takes time to sit down and watch the Super Bowl. President Bill Clinton (center) and daughter Chelsea (with cat Socks) watched Super Bowl XXVII in 1993.

SUPER BOWL V
January 17, 1971
Orange Bowl
Miami, Florida
Baltimore Colts 16
Dallas Cowboys 13

More than 79,000 fans at the Orange Bowl watched the Colts and Cowboys commit 11 turnovers in a sloppy game that finished in an exciting way. Baltimore kicker Jim O'Brien kicked the game-winning 32-yard field goal with five seconds left.

broadcast. The most famous of these appeared during Super Bowl XVIII, when Apple Computer hired motion picture director Ridley Scott to produce a 60-second commercial that resembled a movie. Advertisers have tried to outdo each other ever since.

It's no wonder. The television audience for the Super Bowl is the biggest of the year.

Jim O'Brien

Brand New Titans

The AFL's New York franchise originally was called the Titans. The team changed its name to Jets in 1963. The Tennessee Oilers changed their nickname to Titans in 1999.

The Jets' Mission

New York Jets coach Weeb Ewbank, who had been released as the Colts' coach in 1962, said the AFL's Jets "were playing…for an entire league." In Super Bowl III, Ewbank's Jets defeated the Colts coached by the man who replaced him, Don Shula.

Historic Moments

The Super Bowl has produced some unforgettable moments as it has grown to become America's biggest sporting event. Here are some of the most memorable stories.

Namath's Guarantee

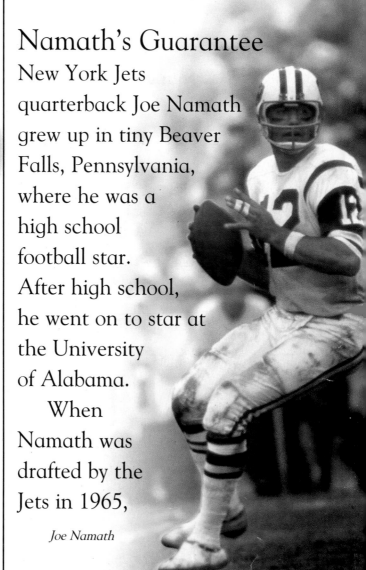

New York Jets quarterback Joe Namath grew up in tiny Beaver Falls, Pennsylvania, where he was a high school football star. After high school, he went on to star at the University of Alabama.

When Namath was drafted by the Jets in 1965,

Joe Namath

however, the small-town boy immediately made himself at home in New York City. Sportswriters started referring to him as Broadway Joe.

At Super Bowl III, Broadway Joe made his biggest splash when he "guaranteed" that the underdog Jets would beat the NFL's Baltimore Colts. Namath's comments received national attention because the Colts were expected to beat the AFL's Jets by three touchdowns or more.

Few outside the Jets' locker room believed New York would win, but Namath's bold prediction came true. Namath, who completed 17 of 28 passes for 206 yards, was named the game's most valuable player.

After the Jets' 16–7 victory, Namath ran off the Orange Bowl field waving his right index finger to tell the world that the Jets were the number-one team in all of pro football.

Roger Staubach

SUPER BOWL VI
January 16, 1972
Tulane Stadium
New Orleans, Louisiana
Dallas Cowboys 24
Miami Dolphins 3

The frustration of losing Super Bowl V helped drive the Cowboys to victory in Super Bowl VI. Dallas quarterback Roger Staubach completed 12 of 19 passes for 119 yards and 2 touchdowns to earn MVP honors.

Presidential Playbook
President Richard Nixon called Miami coach Don Shula to suggest a pass play to receiver Paul Warfield against Dallas in Super Bowl VI.

Don Shula

SUPER BOWL VII
January 14, 1973
Memorial Coliseum
Los Angeles,
California
Miami Dolphins 14
Washington Redskins 7

Miami pounded the Redskins, led by Larry Csonka (112 rushing yards), and survived a late comeback bid by Washington to complete the only perfect season in NFL history. Miami safety Jake Scott intercepted 2 passes and was selected most valuable player.

Coach Don Shula enjoyed his first Super Bowl victory. He had been the losing coach in Super Bowls III (with Baltimore) and VI (with Miami).

Dolphins' Perfect Season

Miami players were humbled by their 24–3 loss to the Dallas Cowboys in Super Bowl VI. But instead of letting the defeat get them down, the Dolphins vowed to get better.

On the way to winning the AFC title that earned them a spot in Super Bowl VII, the determined Dolphins won every game they played. Their record was 16–0 when they lined up to play the Washington Redskins in Super Bowl VII.

The Dolphins' offense featured many talented players, including quarterback Bob Griese and wide receiver Paul Warfield. However, Miami's real offensive strength was its running game. Fullback Larry Csonka ran like a powerful bull. Halfbacks Jim Kiick and Eugene (Mercury) Morris were faster and more difficult for defenses to contain.

Super Bowl VII MVP Jake Scott returns an interception.

Miami's defense was known as the "No-Name Defense." It got its nickname from Dallas coach Tom Landry, who said he could not name any of the Dolphins' defensive players. Still, the "No-Name Defense" had plenty of talent, including linebacker Nick Buoniconti, who wound up in the Pro Football Hall of Fame.

The Dolphins showed all their talents against the Washington Redskins in Super Bowl VII, racing to a 14–0 lead and holding on for a 14–7 victory. The 17–0 Dolphins had achieved the NFL's only perfect season.

Larry Csonka

SUPER BOWL VIII
January 13, 1974
Rice Stadium
Houston, Texas
Miami Dolphins 24
Minnesota Vikings 7

The Dolphins became the second team to win back-to-back Super Bowls with a victory over Minnesota. Miami fullback Larry Csonka rushed for 145 yards on 33 carries and scored 2 touchdowns to earn MVP honors.

SUPER BOWL IX
January 12, 1975
Tulane Stadium
New Orleans,
Louisiana
Pittsburgh Steelers 16
Minnesota Vikings 6

After a 12–2 season—their best ever—the Pittsburgh Steelers finally made it to their first Super Bowl. Running back Franco Harris, the game's MVP, rushed for a Super Bowl-record 158 yards.

Franco Harris

Steel Curtain
Pittsburgh's defensive front four—Mean Joe Greene, Ernie Holmes, Dwight White, and L.C. Greenwood—were known as the Steel Curtain.

Rooney's Championship

Art Rooney had owned the Pittsburgh Steelers franchise for 42 years before the team made it to its first title game. He was perhaps the most popular and least successful owner in the league.

Rooney finally tasted success during the 1970s, when his Steelers won four Super Bowls in six seasons—dominating the NFL.

Rooney founded the Pittsburgh football team in 1933, when they were known as the Pirates. He changed the name of the team to the Steelers in 1940 to honor the heritage of Pittsburgh's steel industry.

In 1969, the Steelers finished in last place with a record of 1–13, but Rooney and coach Chuck Noll worked hard to improve the team. Five seasons later, Pittsburgh defeated the Minnesota Vikings in Super Bowl IX, and Rooney was presented the Vince Lombardi Trophy.

The Steelers would go on to defeat Dallas 21–17 in Super Bowl X and become the third team (along with Green Bay and Miami) to win back-to-back Super Bowls. Pittsburgh also won Super Bowls XIII (35–31 over Dallas) and XIV (31–19 over the Rams) to become the first team to win four Super Bowls.

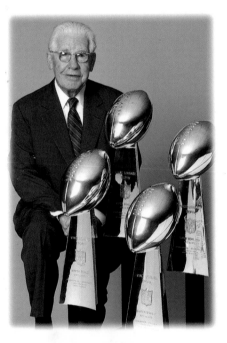
Art Rooney had to wait a long time, but he wound up with four Super Bowl titles.

After Art Rooney died in 1988, his son Dan took over operation of the Steelers. Father and son are both enshrined in the Pro Football Hall of Fame.

Lynn Swann

SUPER BOWL X
January 18, 1976
Orange Bowl
Miami, Florida
Pittsburgh Steelers 21
Dallas Cowboys 17

The Steelers outlasted the Cowboys in one of the most exciting Super Bowls.

Pittsburgh receiver Lynn Swann, who made 2 spectacular receptions, was named most valuable player after catching 4 passes for 161 yards and 1 touchdown.

Quite a Catch
In Super Bowl X, Dallas cut the Steelers' lead to 21–17 on a 34-yard scoring grab by receiver Percy Howard. It was the only catch of Howard's NFL career.

SUPER BOWL XI
January 9, 1977
Rose Bowl
Pasadena, California
Oakland Raiders 32
Minnesota Vikings 14

The Raiders, losers in Super Bowl II, ended nine years of frustration (they had lost six AFL or AFC Championship Games to the eventual Super Bowl winner) by returning to the big game and routing Minnesota. Oakland's Clarence Davis ran for 137 yards on just 16 carries, and Raiders receiver Fred Biletnikoff was named most valuable player after making 4 key receptions for 79 yards.

Fred Biletnikoff

Williams' Breakthrough

When Doug Williams was drafted by the Tampa Bay Buccaneers in 1978, he faced not only the task of proving he could play in the NFL but also the challenge of being one of pro football's few African-American quarterbacks. Williams never played in a Super Bowl during his five seasons as a member of the Buccaneers, but he was a groundbreaker in Super Bowl XXII— as a member of the Washington Redskins.

On the Redskins' first play from scrimmage, Williams became the first African-American to start at quarterback in a Super Bowl. In the second quarter, he set a Super Bowl record by throwing 4 touchdown passes in one quarter.

His touchdown passes of 80, 27, 50, and 8 yards helped the Redskins to a Super Bowl-record 35 points in one quarter. They overpowered the Denver Broncos 42–10.

Williams passed for 340 yards and was named the game's most valuable player—all just one day after undergoing root canal surgery.

After the game, Williams hugged Eddie Robinson, his coach at Grambling State—the winningest college coach ever. Williams

Doug Williams

remembered Robinson's words from his days at Grambling, when his coach told him to "just be the best quarterback you can, and be so good that nobody can ignore you."

Co-MVP Harvey Martin sacks Morton

SUPER BOWL XII
January 15, 1978
Louisiana Superdome
New Orleans,
Louisiana
Dallas Cowboys 27
Denver Broncos 10

Dallas was expected to be in Super Bowl XII. Denver was not. The Broncos owed their success to a defense nicknamed the "Orange Crush," but it was the Cowboys' defense that excelled in Super Bowl XII. Led by co-MVPs Harvey Martin and Randy White, the Cowboys pressured Denver quarterback Craig Morton into throwing 4 interceptions.

Great Indoors
Super Bowl XII, in the Louisiana Superdome, was the first Super Bowl played indoors.

SUPER BOWL XIII
January 21, 1979
Orange Bowl
Miami, Florida
Pittsburgh Steelers 35
Dallas Cowboys 31

Three years after meeting in Super Bowl X, the Cowboys and Steelers met again—with a similar outcome. Most valuable player Terry Bradshaw completed 17 passes for a Super Bowl-record 318 yards and 4 touchdowns to help the Steelers outlast the Cowboys and become the first three-time Super Bowl winners.

Big Play
Tony Dungy, a defensive back for the Steelers, made one of the biggest plays in Super Bowl XIII. Dungy forced a fumble that Pittsburgh recovered and converted into a touchdown for a 35–17 lead. Today, of course, Dungy is better known as the coach of the Indianapolis Colts.

Elway's Elusive Victory

John Elway didn't have any trouble earning the right to play in a Super Bowl—he guided the Denver Broncos to Super Bowls XXI, XXII, and XXIV—but after three losses in three tries, he must have wondered if he would ever win the league's biggest game. In his fourth Super Bowl attempt, Elway finally tasted victory.

Against the Green Bay Packers in Super Bowl XXXII, Elway passed for 123 yards and ran for a touchdown, but it was his trademark ability to lead his team to victory late in the game that clinched his first Super Bowl win. With the game tied

John Elway

24–24 with three and a half minutes remaining, Elway led the Broncos 49 yards in 5 plays to the game-winning touchdown.

Earlier in the game, the quarterback had inspired his teammates by diving headlong into two charging Packers defenders to convert a first down on an important third-and-six situation.

Elway didn't stop with one Super Bowl victory. One year later, he passed for 336 yards while leading Denver to a 34–19 victory over Atlanta in Super Bowl XXXIII. He was named the Super Bowl MVP.

Elway retired a few months later, ending his 16-year NFL career with 51,475 passing yards and 300 touchdown passes. He retired as the NFL's all-time winningest starting quarterback, having won 148 of the 231 games (64.3 percent) in which he started.

SUPER BOWL XIV
January 20, 1980
Rose Bowl
Pasadena, California
Pittsburgh Steelers 31
Los Angeles Rams 19

The defending Super Bowl-champion Steelers found Los Angeles to be tougher than expected, but a late surge led by quarterback Terry Bradshaw saved the day. Bradshaw completed 14 passes for 309 yards and 2 touchdowns and was named MVP as the Steelers became the first team to win four Super Bowls.

Terry Bradshaw

Jim Plunkett

SUPER BOWL XV
January 25, 1981
Louisiana Superdome
New Orleans,
Louisiana
Oakland Raiders 27
Philadelphia Eagles 10

Oakland did not win the AFC Western Division title, but that didn't stop the Raiders, who became the first wild-card playoff team to win a Super Bowl.

Quarterback Jim Plunkett earned MVP honors after completing 13 of 21 passes for 261 yards and 3 touchdowns, including an 80-yard scoring pass to halfback Kenny King that was the longest play in Super Bowl history.

Patriotism on Display

Less than five months after the terrorist attacks of September 11, 2001, the NFL paid tribute to America's patriotism at Super Bowl XXXVI in New Orleans.

Coincidentally, the New England Patriots were the AFC representative in the NFL's biggest game, facing the St. Louis Rams.

American flags were on display throughout the city. Red, white, and blue banners decorated the stadium grounds. Security was tight, but spirits were high during Super Bowl week.

Policemen and firefighters who had performed heroically in rescue efforts were honored before the game.

After losing three of their first four regular-season games, the Patriots were surprise contenders in the Super Bowl, but young quarterback Tom Brady and an effective defense had propelled them through the AFC playoffs. Still, they weren't expected to defeat the high-scoring Rams, led by Kurt Warner.

The Patriots—wearing red, white, and blue uniforms—returned an interception for a touchdown, and Brady's 8-yard touchdown pass to David Patten gave New England a 14–3 lead at halftime.

After the Rams tied the score 17–17 with just 1:30 remaining, Brady led the Patriots on a game-winning 53-yard drive. As time ran out, Adam Vinatieri kicked a 48-yard field goal to win the game.

The Patriots celebrated as red, white, and blue confetti floated from the ceiling of the Louisiana Superdome.

Tom Brady

SUPER BOWL XVI
January 24, 1982
Silverdome
Pontiac, Michigan
San Francisco 49ers 26
Cincinnati Bengals 21

The 49ers and Bengals, who both had 6–10 records only a year earlier, made their first appearance in a Super Bowl. San Francisco quarterback Joe Montana, who completed 14 passes for 157 yards and 1 touchdown, was named MVP. Behind Montana, the 49ers built a 20–0 lead, and then San Francisco relied upon its defense to hold off Cincinnati's late charge.

Joe Montana

John Riggins

SUPER BOWL XVII
January 30, 1983
Rose Bowl
Pasadena, California
Washington Redskins 27
Miami Dolphins 17

The Dolphins scored first, but Miami's so-called "Killer B's" defense could not contain Redskins running back John Riggins, who scored the go-ahead touchdown on a 43-yard run and rushed for a Super Bowl-record 166 yards.

Walker's Race
The Dolphins' Fulton Walker became the first player in Super Bowl history to return a kickoff for a touchdown when he ran one back 98 yards in game XVII.

Super Bowl Superstars

Great Super Bowl performances have lifted NFL players to superstar status. Here are some of the players who have earned a place in history.

Bart Starr

Super Bowls I, II

Bart Starr's statistics do not tell the whole story behind his value to the Green Bay Packers in Super Bowls I and II. He completed 29 of 47 attempts (a rate of 62 percent) for 452 yards and 3 touchdowns in those two games, but he did so much more.

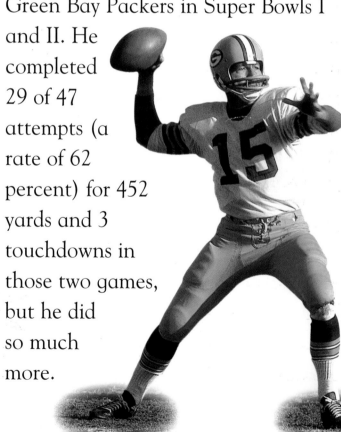

Starr was an on-field leader, who ran the Packers' offense the way coach Vince Lombardi wanted. He was a good play caller who made smart decisions about how to attack opponents. In Super Bowl I, the Packers were successful on 11 of 15 third-down conversions.

Starr, who stood 6 feet 1 inch and weighed 197 pounds, was born in Montgomery, Alabama, and played college football at the University of Alabama. He was not flashy, but he made few mistakes in his two Super Bowl performances. He was named the most valuable player in both games.

Starr's steady, efficient play—especially in big games—was one of the biggest reasons he was elected to the Pro Football Hall of Fame in 1977.

Bart Starr nearly always came up big in big games.

Marcus Allen

SUPER BOWL XVIII
January 22, 1984
Tampa Stadium
Tampa, Florida
Los Angeles Raiders 38
Washington Redskins 9

John Riggins' Super Bowl rushing record lasted only one year. Raiders running back Marcus Allen gained 191 yards against the NFL's top-ranked rush defense, highlighted by a 74-yard score, to earn MVP honors

At Last, L.A.
The Raiders' Super Bowl victory was the first for a Los Angeles team. The Raiders, now in Oakland, were located in Los Angeles from 1982–1994.

SUPER BOWL XIX
January 20, 1985
Stanford Stadium
Stanford, California
San Francisco 49ers 38
Miami Dolphins 16

Running back Roger Craig gained 135 total yards and scored 3 times for the 49ers, but quarterback Joe Montana, who passed for 331 yards and 3 touchdowns, was voted the game's most valuable player. He joined Bart Starr and Terry Bradshaw as the only two-time Super Bowl MVPs.

Dan's Last Stand
NFL all-time passing yards leader Dan Marino played in Super Bowl XIX during his second season in the league, but that was the only Super Bowl he appeared in during his 17-year career.

Dan Marino

Terry Bradshaw

Super Bowls IX, X, XIII, XIV

Dallas Cowboys linebacker Thomas Henderson taunted Terry Bradshaw before Super Bowl XIII, questioning his intelligence. Henderson said that the Steelers' quarterback could not spell "cat" even if you "spotted him the *c* and the *a*." Bradshaw obviously knew how to spell "win."

Bradshaw grew up in Shreveport, Louisiana, and played college football at Louisiana Tech. Steelers fans expected big things after the club selected the 6-foot 3-inch, 215-pound quarterback with the first pick of the 1970 NFL Draft.

Things didn't go as planned, at least not for the first few years, as Bradshaw struggled. Finally, in 1974, he took over as the full-time starter and led Pittsburgh to four Super Bowl victories in six seasons.

In Super Bowl XIII, his third Super Bowl, he passed for 318 yards and 4 touchdowns to beat Dallas. The next year, in Super Bowl XIV, he became the first player to pass for 300 yards in two Super Bowls while leading the Steelers over the Rams. He earned MVP honors in both games and was inducted into the Pro Football Hall of Fame in 1989.

Richard Dent

SUPER BOWL XX
January 26, 1986
Louisiana Superdome
New Orleans, Louisiana
Chicago Bears 46
New England Patriots 10

A rock-solid defense propelled the 1985 Chicago Bears to a 15–1 record and recognition as one of the NFL's all-time best teams. Led by MVP defensive end Richard Dent, they thoroughly dominated New England to win the franchise's first Super Bowl.

Chicago built a 23–3 halftime lead behind a huge edge in total yards (the Bears gained 236 yards to minus-19 for the Patriots in the first half). Chicago scored 21 third-quarter points to take a 44–3 lead.

Terry Bradshaw

Phil Simms

SUPER BOWL XXI
January 25, 1987
Rose Bowl
Pasadena, California
New York Giants 39
Denver Broncos 20

Quarterback Phil Simms, the game's MVP, produced a record-breaking day while leading the Giants to their first NFL title in 30 years. Simms completed 22 of 25 pass attempts for 268 yards and 3 touchdowns, setting Super Bowl records for consecutive completions (10) and completion percentage (88 percent).

Jim Plunkett

Super Bowls XV, XVIII

Oakland Raiders quarterback Jim Plunkett began the 1980 season on the bench. He ended it as the most valuable player of Super Bowl XV, a performance that capped one of the NFL's greatest comeback stories.

Jim Plunkett

Plunkett, who grew up in the San Francisco Bay Area, played football for Stanford University, where he won the 1970 Heisman Trophy. After the New England Patriots selected him with the first pick of the 1971 NFL Draft, Plunkett earned rookie of the year honors.

But Plunkett, playing for bad teams, struggled after that. In 1976, the Patriots traded him to San Francisco, where he played two years before the 49ers released him.

The Raiders signed him in 1978, where he sat on the bench. Finally, in 1980, Plunkett replaced an injured Dan Pastorini in week 5 and led the Raiders to 13 wins in 15 games.

Plunkett passed for 261 yards and 3 touchdowns in a 27–10 victory in Super Bowl XV. In Super Bowl XVIII, he passed for 172 yards and a touchdown in the Raiders' 38–9 victory over Washington.

SUPER BOWL XXII
January 31, 1988
Jack Murphy Stadium
San Diego, California
Washington Redskins 42
Denver Broncos 10

The Broncos jumped out to a 10–0 lead before the Redskins' offense woke up and made Super Bowl history. Quarterback Doug Williams, voted most valuable player, passed for 340 yards and 4 touchdowns, and running back Timmy Smith rushed for a Super Bowl-record 204 yards. The Redskins scored a Super Bowl-record 35 points in the second quarter.

Super Rookie Sub
Redskins rookie running back Timmy Smith, who had only 29 rushing attempts during the 1987 regular season, did not know he would start Super Bowl XXII (in place of the injured George Rogers) until just before kickoff.

Bill Walsh

SUPER BOWL XXIII
January 22, 1989
Joe Robbie Stadium
Miami, Florida
San Francisco 49ers 20
Cincinnati Bengals 16

Joe Montana faced an unusual situation—the 49ers were behind late in a Super Bowl—but he reacted in usual fashion. Montana led the 49ers on a 92-yard drive in 11 plays, capped by his 10-yard touchdown pass to John Taylor with 34 seconds remaining, making San Francisco the champs. Montana completed 23 of 36 passes for 357 yards and 2 touchdowns. Jerry Rice, who caught 11 passes for 215 yards and 1 touchdown, was named most valuable player.

Joe Montana

Super Bowls XVI, XIX, XXIII, XXIV

Joe Montana is considered one of the best quarterbacks in NFL history at least partly because he played so well under pressure—especially in the Super Bowl.

The San Francisco 49ers did not select Montana, a star at Notre Dame, until the third round of the 1979 draft, but he played as if he were a number-one pick throughout his Pro Football Hall of Fame career. He never lost a Super Bowl

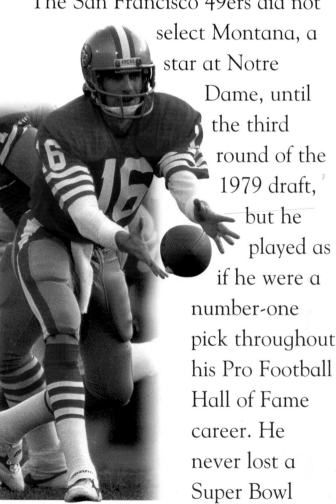

Joe Montana

game and produced some of the most famous plays in history.

In Super Bowl XXIII, with the 49ers trailing the Cincinnati Bengals 16–13 in the final minutes of the game, Montana led his team 92 yards in 11 plays, ending with his winning 10-yard touchdown pass to wide receiver John Taylor with 34 seconds left. Montana finished the game with 357 passing yards.

Montana averaged 286 passing yards and passed for 11 touchdowns in four Super Bowl victories, including a record 5 touchdown passes against the Denver Broncos in Super Bowl XXIV. The 49ers won that game 55–10.

Remarkably, he threw no interceptions while attempting 122 passes in Super Bowl competition. Montana is the only player to be named Super Bowl MVP on three occasions (XVI, XIX, XXIV).

SUPER BOWL XXIV
January 28, 1990
Louisiana Superdome
New Orleans, Louisiana
San Francisco 49ers 55
Denver Broncos 10

Joe Montana completed 22 of 29 passes for 297 yards and 5 touchdowns to earn his third Super Bowl MVP award. The 49ers' margin of victory was the largest in Super Bowl history.

Busted Broncos
The Broncos' loss in Super Bowl XXIV was the franchise's fourth without a win, tying Minnesota for the worst all-time record.

SUPER BOWL XXV
January 27, 1991
Tampa Stadium
Tampa, Florida
New York Giants 20
Buffalo Bills 19

In one of the best-played Super Bowls, the Giants edged the Bills as Buffalo's Scott Norwood missed a 47-yard field goal with 4 seconds left. Giants running back Ottis Anderson ran for 102 yards and a touchdown to earn MVP honors.

Super Singer
During the Persian Gulf War, Whitney Houston delivered one of the Super Bowl's most memorable moments with her rendition of the National Anthem at XXV. A recording of her performance quickly became a hit single that benefited the Gulf Crisis Fund.

Jerry Rice

Super Bowls XXIII, XXIV, XXIX, XXXVII

One of Joe Montana's favorite targets was wide receiver Jerry Rice, believed by many to be the best receiver in NFL history.

After the 6–2, 196-pound

Jerry Rice

receiver was drafted out of Mississippi Valley State in 1985, he quickly demonstrated his talent. In his second season, he led the NFL with 1,570 receiving yards. In his third year, he had an NFL-record 22 touchdown catches.

While teamed with Montana, Rice set a Super Bowl record with 215 receiving yards and scored a touchdown in Super Bowl XXIII. He added 3 more touchdown receptions in Super Bowl XXIV. Rice also caught 3 touchdown passes from Steve Young in Super Bowl XXIX.

Eight years later, Rice played in Super Bowl XXXVII as a member of the Oakland Raiders. He caught a touchdown pass from Rich Gannon to extend his Super Bowl record to 8 career touchdown receptions.

Rice also owns the Super Bowl record for most points scored in a career (48).

Mark Rypien

SUPER BOWL XXVI
January 26, 1992
Hubert H. Humphrey Metrodome
Minneapolis, Minnesota
Washington Redskins 37
Buffalo Bills 24

The temperature was freezing outside, but inside the warm Metrodome, the Redskins' Mark Rypien passed for 292 yards and 2 touchdowns to hand the Bills their second successive Super Bowl defeat.

Super Joe
The Redskins' Super Bowl XXVI victory was coach Joe Gibbs' third Super Bowl win—each with a different starting quarterback.

Joe Gibbs

Troy Aikman

SUPER BOWL XXVII
January 31, 1993
Rose Bowl
Pasadena, California
Dallas Cowboys 52
Buffalo Bills 17

Dallas quarterback Troy Aikman completed 22 of 30 passes for 273 yards and 4 touchdowns to win MVP honors and lead the Cowboys to their first Super Bowl victory in 15 years. Buffalo committed a record 9 turnovers.

Emmitt Smith

Super Bowls XXVII, XXVIII, XXX

On his way to setting the NFL career rushing record, Emmitt Smith made a habit of playing for Super Bowl champions.

Smith, a high school and college football star in Florida, was considered small (5–9, 216 pounds) by NFL standards. The Cowboys believed in Emmitt enough to draft him with the seventeenth overall pick in 1990. He helped them improve from a 1–15 record in 1989 to 7–9 in his rookie season. Two seasons later, Smith was playing in his first Super Bowl. Against Buffalo in Super Bowl XXVII, Smith rushed for 108 yards, caught 6 passes, and scored a touchdown.

Cowboys owner Jerry Jones, holding the Lombardi Trophy, celebrates with coach Jimmy Johnson.

Emmitt Smith

Jim Kelly

In Super Bowl XXVIII, Smith rushed for 132 yards and 2 scores against Buffalo, and he was named the game's most valuable player.

The Cowboys returned to the Super Bowl after the 1995 season, again led by Smith. He rushed for 2 scores, giving him a Super Bowl-record 5 career rushing touchdowns, helping Dallas defeat Pittsburgh 27–17. His 1,586 rushing yards are a postseason record.

SUPER BOWL XXVIII
January 30, 1994
Georgia Dome
Atlanta, Georgia
Dallas Cowboys 30
Buffalo Bills 13

Cowboys safety James Washington intercepted a pass and returned a Bills' fumble 46 yards for a touchdown as the Cowboys overcame a 13–6 halftime deficit. Emmitt Smith, the game's MVP, gained 132 yards.

Good News, Bad News
The Buffalo Bills won four consecutive AFC championships from 1990–93—but lost four consecutive Super Bowls.

Steve Young

SUPER BOWL XXIX
January 29, 1995
Joe Robbie Stadium
Miami, Florida
San Francisco 49ers 49
San Diego Chargers 26

Quarterback Steve Young, who had been in Joe Montana's shadow for much of his career, stepped into the spotlight by passing for a record 6 touchdowns to earn MVP honors.

First Time's a Charm
When George Seifert led the 49ers to victory in Super Bowl XXIV, he became only the second coach to win a Super Bowl in his first season. Don McCafferty also accomplished the feat with the Baltimore Colts in Super Bowl V.

Greatest Teams
Green Bay Packers
Won Super Bowls I, II, XXXI

When the Super Bowl was born, the Green Bay Packers carried the burden of proving the NFL's superiority over the rival AFL.

The Packers, a team based in a small Wisconsin city, reflected that region's blue-collar work ethic. Several of the Packers' players were among the NFL's best, but few could be considered flashy. Under the demanding direction of coach Vince Lombardi, the Packers of the 1960s

were already legends, having won three NFL championships before the Super Bowl was born.

Quarterback Bart Starr led the Packers' offense, but the strength of the unit was up front, where Bill Curry, Forrest Gregg, Jerry Kramer, and Fuzzy Thurston formed one of football's greatest offensive lines.

The Packers' defense, led by linebacker Ray Nitschke, end Willie Davis, and cornerback Herb Adderley, was as good if not better than the offense.

Even Packers backups played key roles. Wide receiver Max McGee, an emergency replacement for injured Boyd Dowler, had 7 receptions and scored 2 touchdowns in Super Bowl I.

The Packers' team approach helped them dominate the Kansas City Chiefs in Super Bowl I and the Oakland Raiders in Super Bowl II.

In January 1997, Green Bay won its third Super Bowl behind Brett Favre, a worthy successor to the club's legacy.

Larry Brown

SUPER BOWL XXX
January 28, 1996
Sun Devil Stadium
Tempe, Arizona
Dallas Cowboys 27
Pittsburgh Steelers 17

The Cowboys' so-called "triplets"—Troy Aikman, Emmitt Smith, and Michael Irvin—won their third Super Bowl in four seasons, with help from cornerback Larry Brown, who had 2 key interceptions. Brown was named the game's MVP.

Super Healer
Pittsburgh cornerback Rod Woodson, who badly injured his knee in the first game of the 1995 season, returned to play in Super Bowl XXX, the first Super Bowl of his nine-year career.

Desmond Howard

SUPER BOWL XXXI
January 26, 1997
Louisiana Superdome
New Orleans,
Louisiana
Green Bay Packers 35
New England Patriots 21

Desmond Howard returned a kickoff 99 yards for a score and Brett Favre passed for 2 touchdowns and ran for another as the Packers won their first Super Bowl in 29 years. Howard, the game's MVP, equaled a Super Bowl record with 244 total return yards.

Super Play
Brett Favre's 81-yard touchdown pass to Antonio Freeman against the Patriots in Super Bowl XXXI is the longest scoring pass in Super Bowl history.

Miami Dolphins

Won Super Bowls VII, VIII

The Miami Dolphins made it to the Super Bowl in 1971, just their sixth season as a team. Though they lost that game, the young franchise went on to have two of the NFL's most dominating seasons.

In 1972, Miami won all 17 of its games, including a 14–7 victory over the Washington Redskins in Super Bowl VII. It was the only perfect season in NFL history.

Coach Don Shula's team wasn't finished. The Dolphins repeated as

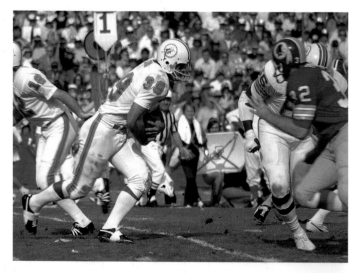

Csonka's power running helped the Dolphins dominate.

champions by beating Minnesota in Super Bowl VIII—their third consecutive Super Bowl.

The Dolphins' offense was led by quarterback Bob Griese and fullback Larry Csonka. While Csonka gained yards pounding the middle, halfbacks Jim Kiick and Eugene (Mercury) Morris ran around the ends. Griese's favorite receivers were Paul Warfield and Howard Twilley.

Miami's "No-Name Defense" featured few stars but dominated opponents, thanks to talented players such as linebacker Nick Buoniconti, linemen Manny Fernandez and Bill Stanfill, and safeties Dick Anderson and Jake Scott.

Buoniconti, Csonka, Griese, Warfield, center Jim Langer, and guard Larry Little were elected to the Pro Football Hall of Fame, as was Shula, who finished with 347 career victories, the most ever.

SUPER BOWL XXXII
January 25, 1998
Qualcomm Stadium
San Diego, California
Denver Broncos 31
Green Bay Packers 24

Quarterback John Elway, playing in his fourth Super Bowl, finally won one as he led the Broncos on a 49-yard, fourth-quarter drive to the winning touchdown. The victory was the Broncos' first in five tries in the Super Bowl and prevented Green Bay from repeating as Super Bowl champions.

Hometown Advantage

Denver running back Terrell Davis rushed for 157 yards and a Super Bowl-record 3 scores to earn MVP honors— in his hometown of San Diego.

Terrell Davis

John Elway

SUPER BOWL XXXIII
January 31, 1999
Pro Player Stadium
Miami, Florida
Denver Broncos 34
Atlanta Falcons 19

John Elway passed for 336 yards and ran for a touchdown to give the Broncos back-to-back Super Bowl wins. It was Elway's last game in the NFL, and he was named MVP.

Regular Visitor
When coach Dan Reeves led the Falcons to Super Bowl XXXIII, it marked his ninth appearance. He played in two and served as an assistant in three (all with the Cowboys), and then led the Broncos to three Super Bowls as head coach.

Pittsburgh Steelers

Won Super Bowls IX, X, XIII, XIV

The Pittsburgh Steelers produced an NFL dynasty in the late 1970s. They won back-to-back Super Bowls in 1974 (IX) and 1975 (X), and again in 1978 (XIII) and 1979 (XIV).

The first step in the Steelers' success was the arrival of coach Chuck Noll in 1969. Then they stocked their team with a series of remarkable draft selections: Joe Greene (1969); Terry Bradshaw and Mel Blount (1970); Jack Ham (1971); Franco Harris (1972); and Lynn Swann, Jack Lambert, John Stallworth, and Mike Webster (1974). All nine players earned spots in the Pro Football Hall of Fame.

Throughout their reign, the Steelers' defense was one of the NFL's best. Greene, a defensive tackle, led the "Steel Curtain" defense that featured linebackers Lambert and

Ham, and cornerback Blount. On offense, the Steelers initially relied on Harris' running.

By the time the Steelers had made it to Super Bowls XIII and XIV, the offense had opened up, relying on Bradshaw's passing to receivers Swann and Stallworth.

From 1972–79, the Steelers had a record of 102–31–1. They were 88–27–1 in the regular season and 14–4 in the playoffs—one of the greatest dynasties in NFL history.

Kurt Warner

SUPER BOWL XXXIV
January 30, 2000
Georgia Dome
Atlanta, Georgia
St. Louis Rams 23
Tennessee Titans 16

The Rams put the final touches on a Cinderella season by edging Tennessee. Rams quarterback Kurt Warner passed for a Super Bowl-record 414 yards to earn MVP honors.

Longest Yard
Tennessee nearly tied the Rams on the final play of Super Bowl XXXIV, but linebacker Mike Jones tackled Titans receiver Kevin Dyson at the 1-yard line as time expired.

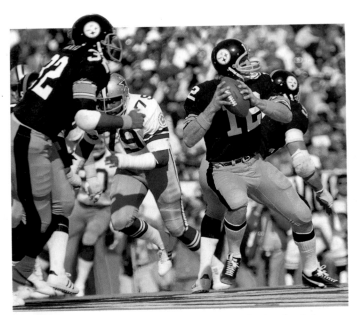

Bradshaw (12) and Harris (32) helped build the Steelers' dynasty.

Ray Lewis

SUPER BOWL XXXV
January 28, 2001
Raymond James
Stadium
Tampa, Florida
Baltimore Ravens 34
New York Giants 7

Baltimore's defense, considered among the best in NFL history, did not allow the Giants' offense to score. New York's only touchdown came on a kickoff return by Ron Dixon—just seconds before Jermaine Lewis did likewise for the Ravens.

Shufflin' Bears
How bold were the 1985 Bears? They filmed a video called "Super Bowl Shuffle" seven weeks *before* Super Bowl XX. It was all in fun, and was for a good cause— proceeds went to feed the homeless.

Chicago Bears

Won Super Bowl XX

The Chicago Bears won only one Super Bowl—after the 1985 season— but they were unforgettable. They used a ferocious defense and cast of colorful personalities to capture the nation's attention, and they didn't disappoint in Super Bowl XX.

The Bears' 15–1 regular-season record featured many lopsided games. They outscored opponents 456–198. Many fans believe that this Bears team, coached by Mike Ditka, was the NFL's best ever.

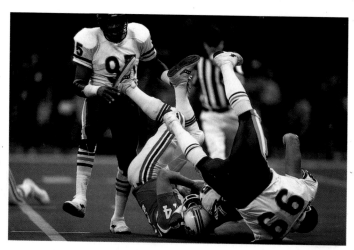

The 1985 Bears beat opponents by an average score of 29–12.

Chicago's defense, led by coordinator Buddy Ryan, surely ranks among the league's best.

Linebacker Mike Singletary and linemen Richard Dent and Dan Hampton led a unit that posted four shutouts, including playoff victories over the Giants and Rams.

The Bears' offense was led by running back Walter Payton, the NFL's all-time leading rusher, and quarterback Jim McMahon. Chicago also had William (Refrigerator) Perry, a 340-pound defensive tackle who lined up as a fullback in short-yardage situations.

The Bears demolished the Patriots 46–10 in Super Bowl XX. Perry even scored a touchdown to help Chicago build what was then the largest margin of victory in Super Bowl history. Dent, one of many defensive stars, was named most valuable player.

SUPER BOWL XXXVI
February 3, 2002
Louisiana Superdome
New Orleans, Louisiana
New England Patriots 20
St. Louis Rams 17

Second-year quarterback Tom Brady led the Patriots to the the game-winning field goal as New England upset the heavily favored Rams. St. Louis had 3 turnovers in the face of a hounding Patriots defense. Brady was named most valuable player.

Adam Vinatieri (4)

Clutch Kick
New England kicker Adam Vinatieri kicked the game-winning 48-yard field goal in Super Bowl XXXVI—the first time a final-play score decided a Super Bowl.

Brad Johnson

SUPER BOWL
XXXVII
January 26, 2003
Qualcomm Stadium
San Diego, California
Tampa Bay Buccaneers 48
Oakland Raiders 21

Tampa Bay's defense intercepted 5 passes—returning 3 for touchdowns—as the Buccaneers won their first Super Bowl. Quarterback Brad Johnson passed for 2 touchdowns, while Tampa Bay safety Dexter Jackson, who had 2 interceptions, was named MVP.

Cause For Celebration
Nobody enjoyed Tampa Bay's Super Bowl victory more than the club's fans, who had endured many bad seasons and a 26-game losing streak.

San Francisco 49ers

Won Super Bowls XVI, XIX, XXIII, XXIV, XXIX

The San Francisco 49ers are tied with the Dallas Cowboys for most Super Bowl victories with five. Four of their titles came between the 1981 and 1989 seasons.

How did the 49ers win four Super Bowls in nine seasons? Start with an offensive system that almost every team has copied, add in one of the greatest quarterbacks (Joe Montana) in NFL history and one of the greatest receivers (Jerry Rice), and you have the team of the 1980s.

Coach Bill Walsh's innovative "West Coast" offense helped the 49ers reach the playoffs in 1981. They defeated Cincinnati 26–21 in Super Bowl XVI as Montana won the first of his three Super Bowl MVP awards.

The 49ers went on to win three more Super Bowls during the decade,

the last two (XXIII and XXIV) with Rice catching passes from Montana.

The 49ers added a fifth title when Steve Young passed for a record 6 touchdowns in Super Bowl XXIX. Rice caught 3 touchdown passes, and Young was named MVP.

The 49ers' defense also played a key role in the team's success. Defensive back Ronnie Lott, the leader of that unit, was enshrined in the Pro Football Hall of Fame the same year (2000) as Montana.

SUPER BOWL XXXVIII
February 1, 2004
Reliant Stadium
Houston, Texas

The Super Bowl will return to Houston for the first time in 30 years for Super Bowl XXXVIII. The only previous Super Bowl in the area was played at Rice Stadium.

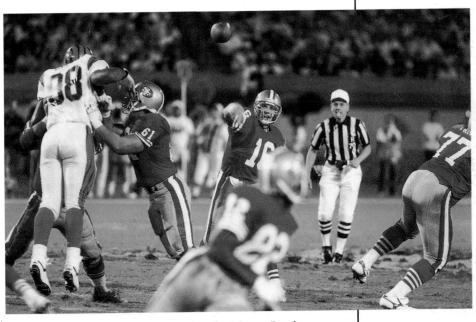

Joe Montana was never intercepted in four Super Bowl games.

San Francisco 49ers

Dallas Cowboys

The Cowboys won three Super Bowls with Troy Aikman (8) and Emmitt Smith (22).

Dallas Cowboys

Won Super Bowls VI, XII, XXVII, XXVIII, XXX

Legendary coach Tom Landry and star quarterback Roger Staubach were the key figures when the Cowboys won Super Bowls VI and XII. Fifteen years later, a new cast led Dallas to NFL championships.

In 1989, Jimmy Johnson replaced Landry and began building a young team that would go on to win Super Bowls XXVII and XXVIII.

Those Cowboys were known for a triple-threat offense led by the passing of quarterback Troy Aikman to receiver Michael Irvin, and the rushing of running back Emmitt Smith. Tight end Jay Novacek gave Aikman another fine receiving target, as he demonstrated with touchdown receptions in Super Bowls XXVII and XXX.

The Cowboys' defense, though not as glamorous, was equally effective, thanks to players such as end Charles Haley, linebacker Ken Norton Jr., and safety Darren Woodson.

Barry Switzer replaced Johnson, who left the Cowboys after five seasons (1989–1993). Switzer coached Dallas to a victory over Pittsburgh in Super Bowl XXX. The victory made the Cowboys the only team in history to win three Super Bowls in four seasons.

Lamar Hunt

Super Name
AFL Kansas City Chiefs owner Lamar Hunt was the first to call the AFL-NFL Championship Game the Super Bowl. The name was used by the media at the first Super Bowl, but did not appear on game tickets for two more years.

Super Conference
Of the first 37 Super Bowls, NFL/NFC teams have won 21. During one stretch (XIX-XXXI), the NFC won 13 games in a row.

Glossary

AFC
The American Football Conference, consisting of 16 of the NFL's 32 teams.

Commissioner
The leader of the NFL.

Completion
A forward pass that is thrown and caught by the offense.

Draft
The annual selection of college players by NFL teams.

Dynasty
A period of time during which one team is especially successful.

Heisman Trophy
The award presented annually to college football's best player.

Interception
A pass intended for an offensive player that is caught by a defender.

Media
Members of news organizations, including reporters and photographers.

Merger
When the NFL and AFL joined together to become one league.

Most Valuable Player
The player who had the biggest impact in a game or a season.

NFC
The National Football Conference, consisting of 16 of the NFL's 32 teams.

Playoffs
Games played after the regular season to determine the league champion.

Pro Football Hall of Fame
A museum in Canton, Ohio (birthplace of the NFL), where the game's greatest players are honored.

Roman Numerals
All Super Bowls are identified by numbers created by the ancient Romans. Here are some examples and what they represent:

Super Bowl	Number
I	1
II	2
III	3
IV	4
V	5
VI	6
VII	7
VIII	8
IX	9
X	10
XX	20
XXX	30
XL	40
L	50

Underdog
A team that is not expected to win.

Vince Lombardi Trophy
The trophy presented to the team that wins the Super Bowl, named in honor of the legendary Green Bay Packers coach.

Wild Card
A team that makes the playoffs without winning its division.

Index